I0845184

Chapter One: Introduction to Financial Literacy

Section A: Definition and Importance

What is Financial Literacy?

Financial literacy serves as a basis for rational and informed decision-making concerning one's financial needs. It is more than just knowing about budgeting or saving, it means one has a broad knowledge of financial terms and ideas in practice. This chapter will introduce you to the basics of financial literacy so that you can have a hand in your own financial life.

Why Financial Literacy Matters

For many reasons, it's important to understand and use financial knowledge. It gives you the information and skills you need to:

- **Handle Daily Finances**: Learn how to handle daily costs, make budgets, and choose wisely what to spend your money on.
- **Build Wealth**: Come up with plans for how to save, spend, and get rich over time.
- **Reduce Risks**: Know what the financial risks are and how to deal with them to make sure you have a safe financial future.
- **Make Smart Choices**: Give yourself the information and tools you need to make smart choices about your money that are in line with your values and goals.

Section B: Personal Finance Journey - Your Story

Reflecting on Your Financial Journey

Briefly think of your personal financial journey. What has your experience with money been and what lessons have you learned from it? These practical tips are tailored to suit your own specific needs, whether you're simply getting into financial literacy or have encountered some difficulties recently.

The Importance of Sharing Stories

The process of acquiring financial literacy in most cases is often an uncharted journey. Sharing our stories enables us to develop a network that allows people to learn from one's successes and failures. We'll include personal stories and practical scenarios from everyday life to help you relate the financial jargon and apply it to your daily situations.

Section C: Setting the Stage for Financial Empowerment

What to Expect in This Guide

In this guide, there will be an overview of several financial subjects that vary in complexity level, starting from the fundamentals of budgeting and saving and reaching more sophisticated phenomena such as investment, saving for retirement and risk management. The chapters are designed chronologically in such manner that each of them lays foundation for the subsequent one and hence step by step guide to financial empowerment.

Your Role in the Financial Literacy Journey

At this point, your dedication towards learning and implementing the core financial values cannot be undermined. This guide is highly adaptable, intended for use in financial literacy that addresses individuals' distinct situations, interests, and preferences.

Chapter Two: Understanding the Basics

A. Differentiating Between Assets and Liabilities

There are essential things that one needs to understand in the road to financial literacy, among them is asset versus liability definition. This understanding of the difference is basically based on what I have learned about it from the book "Rich dad poor dad" written by Robert T Kiyosaki.

Assets

Building wealth involves accumulating assets over the years. These are items that take money out of your pocket. Assets include real estate properties that generate rental incomes, investment portfolios, as well as business ventures. To do so, the mantra focuses on accumulating appreciating assets or those paying dividends towards wealth independence.

Liabilities

But then, assets are expenditures taken away from your purse whereas liabilities will be out of the purse. Such obligations may include paying mortgages, car loans or any other recurring debt. Kiyosaki stresses on reducing your liabilities and leveraging them correctly to attain income producing assets.

B. The Concept of Passive Income

This brings us to the importance of understanding the concept of passive income, which is the concept that builds upon the foundation of assets. The book talks about passive income which is money gotten without much of effort being put forth from you. It is the income that one reaps from investments, rented houses or business that does not require a lot of active input.

Importance of Passive Income

A passive source of income ensures financial stability and gives more freedom in daily living. A passive source of income ensures financial stability and gives more freedom in daily living. Passive income is a means to financial security and more flexible life choices. Diversification of income sources, and passive streams create financial freedom that is not dependent on traditional employment.

C. Budgeting and Expense Tracking

Lastly, financial literacy involves learning how to manipulate some of these practical tools in the management of your money. As mentioned by various financial guides such as "The Total Money Makeover" by Dave Ramsey, budgeting and expense tracking play a crucial role in attaining financial discipline.

Creating a Budget

A budget is important for determining how income is allocated for different things so that all the money you spend gets justified with an objective. By adopting such a proactive attitude, people can schedule saving, payments for debts, as well as expenses not linked with any objectives first.

Expense Tracking

It is important to monitor expenditures as well. Tracking daily, weekly and monthly expenses gives an idea on one's spending patterns hence pinpointing places of adjustment will be easier. The tracking process becomes easy when one uses tools such as budgeting apps and/or spreadsheet.

Chapter Three: Building a Strong Financial Foundation

I. Introduction

Congratulations on taking the first steps towards learning about money! We've talked about the basics of budgeting, knowing assets and debts. Now let's talk about the most important parts of building a strong financial base..

II. Emergency Fund and Its Significance

A. What is an Emergency Fund?

The emergency fund serves as your financial safety net and provides support against unforeseen expenses. In case of a medical emergency, car breakdown, or even job loss, it is often very important when you have a well-stocked emergency savings account.

B. How Much Should You Save?

It is always advisable for people to save three to six months of their living expenses according to financial experts. The cost is enough to help you get over unexpected situations and at the same time keep your long term objectives intact.

C. Steps to Build and Maintain Your Emergency Fund

1. Make Clear Goals: Write down your financial goals and use your monthly costs to figure out how much you need in your emergency fund.
2. Regular Saving: Make it a habit to put money into your backup fund every month. It's a cost that you can't avoid every month.
3. Separate Account: Keep your emergency fund in a separate account that is easy to get to. So you don't spend money without thinking.
4. Evaluate often: Things in life change, so go back to your emergency fund goals and make changes as required. Celebrate big steps forward, but be flexible.

III. Managing and Eliminating Debt

A. The Debt Snowball Method

Inspired by financial guru Dave Ramsey, the debt snowball method is a systematic approach to paying off debts. Here's how it works:

1. List Your Debts: Compile a list of all your debts, from smallest to largest.
2. Minimum Payments: Continue making minimum payments on all debts.
3. Extra Payments: Allocate any extra funds toward paying off the smallest debt first.
4. Snowball Effect: Once the smallest debt is paid off, roll the amount you were paying on it into the next smallest debt. Repeat until all debts are cleared.

B. Why the Debt Snowball Works

The debt snowball method is based on quick wins, which are good for your mental health because they make your bills go away. It might not be the most mathematically sound way to do things, but the incentive it gives you often outweighs the interest you save.

C. Avoiding Credit Pitfalls and Debt Traps

1. Responsible Credit Use: Do not depend much on credit and do not allow yourself to rack up debts with high interest rates.
2. Understanding Interest Rates: Take note of the interest attached to your debts. To start with, high-interest debt should be paid for first.
3. Emergency Fund as a Preventive Measure: For example, having a good emergency fund is critical so as one avoids taking too expensive loans.

IV. Conclusion

Saving appropriately, properly handling credits, and getting rid of debts are necessary for a strong financial basis establishment. Creating and ensuring that there is an emergency fund as well as managing your debts will go a long way in securing your finances. We will look at economizing in the next chapter and why it is one of life's prerequisites to achieving financial fitness in chapter 5.

Chapter Four: Smart Saving and Frugal Living

A. The Millionaire Mindset - Living Below Your Means

The fact that in their quest for financial literacy they accept a millionaire's perspective is important. The Millionaire Next Door emphasizes that one key component of this wealth accumulation process is making do with little. This does not entail a life of self-denial, but rather an informed choice about how best to utilize resources.

1. Embracing Frugality

Smart savings start with frugality. It is simply deliberate selection on the money outlay aspect. Think about any purchase as important and differentiate between a need and a want. You can channel funds that you would have spent on a large home into savings or investments by embracing a frugal lifestyle.

2. Creating a Budget that Reflects Your Values

Therefore, it is critical to develop a budget, based on the budgetary concepts explained above, and in sync with your personal values. Put resources in the place where you want them most – in educating yourself, having experiences or developing your personality. Developing a good budget indicates the importance of your priorities on your spending.

3. Avoiding Lifestyle Inflation

With increased earnings, there is usually a desire to make equal proportional expenditures. Nevertheless, a person desirous of wealth has to fight against lifestyle inflation. Rather, divert extra money toward saving, investments, and debt reduction. This is a fast way in which one can create wealth while maintaining their standard of living.

B. Importance of Disciplined Saving

1. Establishing Savings Goals

One of the basic steps one needs to take towards ensuring financial securities is saving money. Set realistic and attainable savings targets. Objectives can include saving money for emergency uses, down payment towards building of a new house as well as achieving one goal – vacation in your wildest dream.

2. Automatic Savings Plans

Set-up automated transfers to a savings account in order to have consistent saving. This habit reduces simplicity in the process and savings becomes an essential part of your daily financial routine.

3. Harnessing the Power of Compound Interest

Many financial literacy sources such as "Total Money Makeover" note that one should begin early in order to accumulate the maximum benefit of compound interest. Disciplined saving can really help you to accumulate a lot of compound interest.

C. Making Smart Spending Choices

1. Evaluating Value for Money

Before you buy anything, compare it with what is important to you and how it fits in your budget plan. Is it a temporary sensation of pleasure or a way to take care of yourself in the future? Changing your mind in this way could lead you towards decisions which are directed at your financial prosperity.

2. Seeking Cost-Effective Alternatives

Frugality is not about low-quality. Consider cost effective alternatives and good buying ideas. There are numerous ways to stretch your dollar, including from researching and comparing different prices to using discount and reward cards.

3. Mindful Consumption

Mindful consumption entails being conscious about how your purchases impact the environment and society at large. Think about buying sustainable and ethical products to ensure that in addition to your money, you are also thinking about another aspect apart from yourself.

Chapter V: Investing Principles

A. Introduction to Investing (inspired by "The Little Book of Common Sense Investing")

Time-wise, wealth can be generated through the investment. Although it appears complicated, knowing the elementary can take you into the road of wealth creation. This chapter will outline the basic ideas in investing.

1. Investing vs. Saving:
- Involves investing in assets and expecting returns over some time span.
- The act of saving revolves around putting away money in order to meet the short-term needs or for unexpected events.

2. Risk and Return:
- Learn about the linkage between risk and return. It is a common thing that higher returns mean higher risk of the transaction.
- Differences in the assets or companies can help minimize the associated risks through diversification.

3. The Power of Compound Interest:
- Investing gives you the golden opportunity of using your time as an ally. Your money grows progressively with compounded interest.
- Take advantage of compounding by investing early.

B. Types of Investments (e.g., Index Funds, Retirement Accounts)

1. Index Funds and ETFs:
- Index funds and ETFs may offer low cost exposure to entire markets.
- These make excellent choices for the beginner – they diversify while retaining simplicity.

2. Retirement Accounts:
- Look into tax-favoured retirement savings tools such as 401(k)s or IRAs.
- Enroll in an employer sponsored program, making regular contributions.

3. Stocks and Bonds:
- Basics in stock market (equity) and bond (fixed income) understanding.
- Balance your portfolio by investing in different assets.
-

C. Long-Term Wealth-Building Strategies

1. Setting Investment Goals:
- Set specific short-term and long-term financial goals.
- Ensure that you link your investment strategy to your targets and time frame.

2. Regular Contributions:
- These smaller yet consistent contributions when added up over time may be able to make substantial effects in the marketplace.
- Invest through dollar cost averaging.

3. Periodic Review and Adjustments:
- Keep reassessing your investment portfolio so that it matches your purposes regularly.
- Alter your plan according to fluctuations of your finances and markets.

Chapter VI: Aligning Finances with Values

A. Your Money and Your Life Energy

This chapter goes deeper and gives a glimpse of how your budget affects your vitality which is drawn from "Your Money or Your Life" by Vicki Robin and Joe Dominguez. Knowing what you are giving up your time and energy in order to earn money will completely redefine your take on personal finances.

1. Reflecting on Life Energy Exchange
- Stop for a while and think about what you do at work and how much it cost you to earn some money. Does this exchange affect you in general terms, that is, your sense of well being and completeness?

2. Calculating the True Cost
- Teach yourself how much do you have to work to pay for your purchase. Such an enlightening experience should assist you in making conscious spending choices.ityEngineer: In most cases, he provides very detailed information about particular topics without mentioning his name.

B. Defining Financial Goals

1. The Power of Goal Setting
- The significance of having well-defined financial objectives that are realistic and attainable. Defining what you are saving for-be it towards a dream vacation, owning a house or having a peaceful retirement is important so one knows where he/she is headed.

2. Short-Term and Long-Term Goals
- Know the difference between short-time and long-time financial goals. Balance your finances accordingly and you will be set for that period in future.

C. Creating a Values-Based Spending Plan

1. Identifying Core Values
- Consider your values, aims, and purposes in life. What exactly gives meaning to your life and makes it worth living? Your spending should be in line with these values, so you can have a more meaningful financial experience.

2. Crafting a Personalized Budget

- Create a budget that is based on your priorities. Distribute available resources on what is important in life, but pay your bills, save and invest on a regular basis.

Action Steps:

1. Life Energy Audit:

- Life energy audit will help you understand what you do for living and how it reflects on your own money situation. Point out some changes that should be made in order for your financial decisions to align with what you value.

2. Goal Setting Workshop:

- Participate in a goal-setting session for the preparation of immediate and long-term fiscal goals. Make your goals smaller and more easily achievable to motivate you in order to break these.

3. Values-Based Budgeting Exercise:

- Carry out values-based budgeting whereby you will distribute your financial resources basing on your core values. In doing so, this will form a basis for future financial decisions.

Chapter Seven: Financial Planning for the Future

Section A: Retirement Planning

1. Understanding the Importance of Retirement Planning

Retirement is an extremely critical period in life and it must be considered financially meticulously. This section will examine why it is important to have a retirement plan and how best you can prepare for it financially.

2. Setting Retirement Goals

Determining the lifestyle that you wish to have in retirement, travel plans, and future healthcare needs can help you learn how to define your retirement goals. The next time we will talk about the importance of having goals in making a sustainable retirement plan.

3. Exploring Retirement Accounts

Find out about various retirement plans like 401(k) and IRA and learn how these can lay down the foundation of your retirement nest egg. In this chapter, we'll examine the advantages and disadvantages for each type of account.

Section B: Estate Planning

1. The Basics of Estate Planning

However, estate planning is not only for the wealthy rather it is part of financial planning for everybody. This part will focus on basics of estate planning like Wills, Trust, Asset division etc.

2. Ensuring Your Wishes are Honored

You need to understand that you must make it clear on how you would want your property and belongings distributed when you pass away. In our discussions, we will talk about legal documentations and how it can help in ensuring smooth inheritance to your heirs or beneficiaries.

3. Minimizing Estate Taxes

Get to learn ways, through which you will be in a position to reduce estate tax. We will discuss legal and financial instruments which can ensure your estate and inheritance of your loved ones.

Section C: Importance of Insurance

1. Understanding Insurance Basics

A good financial plan must incorporate insurance as an element. In this part will be introduced basic on many insurance types such as medical, death, and property one.

2. Mitigating Risks with Insurance

Consider how insurance operates like a cushion, granting one financial cover against mishaps. We will talk about the necessity for sufficient insurance and explain how it aids in managing and reducing different dangers.

3. Balancing Cost and Coverage

Strike a balance between the cost of insurance and the amount of the insurance cover. We will show you how to evaluate insurance policies; understand the policy terms; ensure that your insurance portfolio matches your general financial plan.

Chapter VIII: Seeking Professional Guidance

A. The Role of Financial Advisors

As you strive towards financial literacy and stability, this is one step that might prove crucial. This is where financial advisors come into play and help people with making decisions on many matters that are related to their personal finances. Knowing their job and why it is important for you can have a dramatic effect on your finances.

1. What is a Financial Advisor?

This means that financial advisor is a specially trained person, who gives advice related to different spheres of financial planning. This can assist in setting financial targets, creating individual action plan, and navigating investment options. It is essential to identify varying breeds of financial advisors such as CFPs, investment and insurance advisor respectively.

2. When to Consult a Financial Advisor

It is essential for them to understand the importance of seeking professional help at the appropriate time. Consider consulting a financial advisor when:
- In other words, you're encountering significant changes in your life like, marriage, parenting and so on., or when it comes to old age like, marriage, parenthood, retirement).
- In that case, you are not sure of your investment strategy.
- Tax planning becomes complex.
- Estate planning is needed.
- You seek a holistic financial plan catered for your objectives.

B. How to Choose a Financial Advisor

Choosing the right financial advisor is critical. Follow these steps to ensure you find a professional aligned with your needs:

1. Clarify Your Goals and Needs
- Clearly define your financial goals and the specific areas where you need assistance.

2. Credentials and Qualifications
- Look for advisors with recognized certifications such as CFP, ChFC (Chartered Financial Consultant), or CFA (Chartered Financial Analyst).

3. Fee Structure
   - Understand how the advisor is compensated. Fee-only advisors may be more aligned with your interests.

4. Experience and Track Record
   - Inquire about their experience and request references. A proven track record can instill confidence in their abilities.

5. Communication Style
   - Choose an advisor whose communication style matches your preferences. Clear communication is crucial for a successful partnership.

C. Online Tools and Resources

In addition to traditional financial advisors, there is a wealth of online tools and resources to aid in your financial journey:

1. Robo-Advisors
   - Automated investment platforms that use algorithms to create and manage a diversified portfolio based on your risk tolerance and financial goals.

2. Financial Planning Software
   - Tools like Mint, Personal Capital, or YNAB can help you budget, track expenses, and plan for the future.

3. Educational Platforms
   - Take advantage of online courses and educational platforms that offer insights into various financial topics.

Conclusion

Getting professional advice is one of the ways to ensure your future is taken care of financially. The essence here is to match the financial experience of your chosen expert to your expectations for what lies in store. However, during this journey, note that if you engage in a constructive dialogue with your financial advisors, it could become an important tool towards achieving your financial goals.

Chapter Nine: Continuous Learning and Improvement

The learning and adaptation phase during the course on the road to financial literacy is continuous. In doing so, you will find out that keeping abreast of business/economic issues, acquiring more business/finance related education, and reaching out with other people can mean a lot in terms of financial success.

A. Staying Informed About Financial Trends

Finance and knowledge about it is changing dynamically which makes it important for knowing its true nature before making any decision. Ensure that you are informed on economic indicators, market trends, and finance information. There are numerous reliable financial news sources that can be followed, subscription of newsletters, and participating in on line communities for members exchange knowledge about ongoing financial issues. However, this will put you on notice to act swiftly and wisely so that you can achieve your financial objectives.

B. Expanding Financial Literacy Knowledge

Financial literacy is a growing and expansive area. Dig deeper by seeking education materials other than the basic ones. Instead, think of online classes, workshops, and webinars about sophisticated investments approaches, tax issues and retirement wealth plans. Learning new information can be derived from books, podcasts, or TED talks made by financial specialists.

C. Networking and Learning from Others

It's learning from other people's experiences, which is a key element of the 'continuous improvement. Talk to other people interested in the same financial goals as you are, or who have helpful information for you. People will get chances to share thoughts, give opinions, ask questions and also benefit from past successes and mistakes through joining local financial literacy groups, through participating in online forums, or through attending networking events.

Chapter Ten: Sharing Your Financial Journey
Introduction:

Sharing your experiences and life's lessons in this quest for financial literacy can also prove vital in motivating other folks along the same journey. This chapter focuses on how you can record your financial growth, foster a supportive network, and promote financial education amongst your social group.

Section A: Documenting and Reflecting on Your Progress

- **Keeping a Financial Journal**: Begin with writing a journal on your financial goals, weaknesses, and strengths. Examining how far you have come can be very helpful, even motivating.

- **Tracking Milestones**: Such could include paying off some debt, achieving savings objectives, and engaging in smart investments. Reinforce these successful financial habits and celebrate them.

- **Sharing Success Stories**: Try telling such success stories as an example of financial transformation. It is always important to showcase real life examples because other people will feel like this is nothing but normal and everyone can have a chance of succeeding financially.

Section B: Inspiring Others - Building a Supportive Community

- **Creating a Support System**: Hang around with people whose objectives match yours on financial matters. Such could include friends, family, as well as online forums. Tell people about your journey and know how they have been challenged.

- **Organizing Financial Workshops or Meetups**: Conduct workshops or get-together sessions to discuss financial issues. It opens up avenues for discussions, joint learning and reciprocal assistance.

- **Collaborative Goal Setting**: Foster cooperative setting of objectives in your community. By sharing similar financial objectives, employees become motivated and more accountable.

Section C: Encouraging Financial Literacy in Your Circle

- **Promoting Open Conversations**: End up destroying the taboos on cash while having conversations with your community. Initiate discussions about budgeting, savings and investments.

- **Sharing Educational Resources**: Introduce you circle with quality financial tools such as books, articles, online courses. Inform them of the best place to get more money related knowledge to enhance their financial literacy.

- **Offering Practical Tips**: Discuss some practical tips on daily financial choices. It also entails various things such as budgeting, cost cutting, and bargaining for better prices.

Conclusion:

By sharing your financial journey, both in understanding and practice, you will be contributing to other people's financial success. You are creating a good economic environment by noting down how well you are doing; building a support group; and being financially literate. Financial literacy is a joint adventure, so collectively let's construct a more financially literate tomorrow.

Chapter Eleven: Credit Management and Credit Scores

Section A: Understanding Credit Reports and Scores

1. The Importance of Credit Reports
- Your credit report is a comprehensive record of your credit history.
- Understanding the components of a credit report: personal information, credit accounts, payment history, inquiries, and public records.

2. Obtaining and Reviewing Your Credit Report
- Free annual credit reports for major credit bureaus.
- Understanding what the information in your credit report means.
- Addressing errors that occur in your report.

Section B: Building and Maintaining Good Credit

1. The Basics of Good Credit
- The role of credit in financial health.
- Establishing a positive credit history.

2. Responsible Credit Card Use
- Using credit cards wisely to build credit.
- Tips for responsible credit card management.

3. Dangers of High-Interest Debt
- Understanding the risks associated with high-interest debt.
- Strategies for managing and paying down credit card debt.

Section C: Avoiding Credit Pitfalls and Debt Traps

1. Recognizing Warning Signs
- Identifying signs of potential credit troubles.
- The impact of missed payments and late fees on credit scores.

2. Strategies for Avoiding Debt Traps
- Developing a practical budget in order to prevent the occurrence of overspending.
- To reduce reliance on credit for financial setbacks, building an emergency fund.

Chapter Twelve: Taxes and Personal Finance

A. Basic Understanding of Taxation

Basic knowledge on taxes should be understood if one wants to make sound financial choices. Personal finance involves taxes, which are important, and influence numerous components of our financial lives. This section discusses some basic aspects of taxes so as to equip you deal with this important issue of financial management.

1. Types of Taxes

a. Income Tax
- Explanation of how income tax is calculated.
- Different tax brackets and rates.
- Tax deductions and credits available to individuals.

b. Property Tax
- Overview of property taxes and how they are assessed.
- Strategies for managing and potentially reducing property tax liabilities.

c. Sales Tax
- Understanding sales tax and its impact on your purchases.
- Tips for managing and budgeting for sales tax expenses.

2. Tax Forms and Filing

a. Introduction to Common Tax Forms
- Overview of common tax forms, such as W-2, 1099, and 1040.
- Understanding the information each form provides.

b. Filing Status
- Explanation of different filing statuses (single, married filing jointly, head of household, etc.).
- Choosing the right filing status for your situation.

c. Filing Deadlines
- Importance of adhering to tax filing deadlines.
- Consequences of late filing and strategies for avoiding penalties.

B. Tax-Efficient Investing Strategies

1. Capital Gains and Losses
   - Differentiating between short-term and long-term capital gains.
   - Strategies for minimizing capital gains taxes.

2. Tax-Advantaged Investment Accounts
   - Overview of tax-advantaged accounts, such as IRAs and 401(k)s.
   - Maximizing the benefits of these accounts for retirement savings.

3. Tax-Efficient Portfolio Management
   - Strategies for managing your investment portfolio to minimize tax implications.
   - Understanding the impact of dividends and interest on your taxes.

C. Utilizing Tax-Advantaged Accounts

1. Retirement Accounts
   - Exploring the benefits of contributing to retirement accounts.
   - Choosing the right retirement account based on your financial goals.

2. Health Savings Accounts (HSAs)
   - Understanding the tax advantages of HSAs for healthcare expenses.
   - Maximizing the benefits of HSAs for long-term financial planning.

3. Education Savings Accounts
   - Overview of tax-advantaged accounts for education, such as 529 plans.
   - Planning for education expenses with tax considerations in mind.

Chapter XIII: Behavioral Finance and Emotional Aspects of Money

Section A: Recognizing Behavioral Biases in Financial Decision-Making

When making this journey to become financially literate, it is necessary to explore the intriguing area of behavioral finance. The purpose of this section is to elucidate some of the psychological considerations in making decisions concerning finances. Such understanding gives power to your reason and helps you avoid irrational decisions made on the basis of these biases.

1. **Overcoming Confirmation Bias**: People are often inclined towards seeking information that validates their already held beliefs. This may result in bad financial options. Challenge your assumptions about your decisions on finances and be proactive when seeking information from different people to make informed choices.

2. **The Impact of Loss Aversion**: The pain of loss is felt greatly unlike the gain which brings happiness. Come up with strategies for managing loss aversion like establishing reasonable expectations and targeting the future objectives.

3. **Herding Behavior in Financial Markets**: Know the risk of going with the herd without question. Discuss the advantages of individual thought and how it leads to better business-oriented investment decisions.

Section B: Emotional Intelligence in Money Management

Emotional intelligence goes beyond understanding biases, which is essential for effective money management. The next piece looks at how emotions affect financial choices, and offers practical strategies for building emotional stamina.

1. **Emotional Awareness in Financial Decision-Making**: The ability to pick up with these emotions concerning them money. Recognize how emotions influence your financial decisions, and adopt tactics of managing it.

2. **Stress Management in Financial Crisis**: Financial challenges can be stressful. Make a point of looking at some ways of stress management that can help you remain calm and take wise decisions in hard moments.

3. **Communication Skills in Financial Conversations**: Communication is very important in handling of financial issues particularly in marriages. Build communication skills that will enable you to share the financial issues freely and openly with your partner or even family.

Section C: Overcoming Common Financial Fears and Anxieties

A lot of people suffer financial phobia. Here are some common concerns about money which might occur, and ideas for getting past them.

1. **Fear of Investing**: Know that fear of investment is a huge hindrance in building wealth. Education, risk taking, and starting out in little steps at a time.

2. **Anxiety about Debt**: Debt can be a source of anxiety. Explore strategies to tackle debt systematically and develop healthy financial habits to avoid future debt-related stress.

3. **The Fear of Financial Uncertainty**: Financial uncertainty is a common concern. Discover ways to build a financial safety net, set realistic goals, and create a flexible financial plan to navigate uncertainties.

Chapter XIV: Financial Safety Nets and Risk Management

Section A: Insurance Basics - Health, Life, Property

A.1 Understanding the Importance of Insurance

Insurance serves an important financial protection for you, and your family in unforeseeable and usually expensive circumstances. This section will be focused on providing information about basic types of insurance and the role it plays as part of a good financial strategy.

A.2 Health Insurance Essentials

Understanding the intricacies of health insurance is vital for staying healthy. Health insurance 101, includes explaining different types of coverage, deductions, and importance of preventive care, among other things. Knowing what health insurance is allows you to receive medical services conveniently without endangering the budget.

A.3 Securing Your Future with Life Insurance

The life insurance gives support financially to your family members on your death. This subsection will explain life insurance starting with term life, whole life and others. In this course you will learn about your life insurance needs and be able to choose wisely in order to secure your family's life future.

A.4 Shielding Your Assets with Property Insurance

You have made considerable investments into your home and possessions. On the other hand, we will discuss the significance of property insurance which includes home owners insurance, renter's insurance as well as all the coverages available that prevent your properties from any unplanned dangers. Having a good and proper property insurance makes sure that you build your wealth even when adversities strike.

Section B: Emergency Preparedness Beyond the Emergency Fund

B.1 Building a Comprehensive Emergency Plan

An emergency fund will immediately sort out any financial crisis you may encounter. However, as important as it is to have such a fund, another plan just as essential is a wide-ranging emergency preparedness program. Creating a comprehensive emergency management plan that addresses different possible incidents requires readiness of your facility to face any challenge during any time.

B.2 The Role of an Emergency Preparedness Kit

Learn what it takes to put together an emergency preparedness kit. We will discuss some of the items that should be included in your stockpile for such disasters including financial documents and essential supplies. You make a promise, and the kit is a proof that it's sincere.

B.3 Collaborating with Community Resources

However, community resources can go a long way in helping the community during such trying moments. We shall discuss on how to contact community-based centers, public agencies and support groups that may help during a crisis. Knowing about them makes it easier for you to cope with life's difficulties.

Section C: Hedging Against Financial Risks

C.1 Identifying and Assessing Financial Risks

Financial issues entail risk but through active risk management; adverse effects of it could be minimized. Identifying and monitoring financial risks which include investment risks such as market volatility to job insecurity. Knowing how these risks work helps you be able to make the right decisions and create the right strategies of preventing them.

C.2 Diversification and Risk Reduction Strategies

Look into using diversification as a way to reduce risks within your financial portfolio. Spreading investments into several assets will help you to reduce the negative effects of the market fluctuations and enhance the sustainability of your overall financial approach.

C.3 Insurance as a Risk Mitigation Tool

We will however also explore how individual insurance products can be used in managing risk. Understanding these options like from disability insurance and liability coverage helps you to protect your wealth.

Chapter XV: Ethical and Sustainable Investing

Section 1: Incorporating Ethical Considerations into Investment Decisions

In the dynamic world of finance, ethical considerations have become increasingly important for investors. This section explores how aligning your investments with your values can be a powerful and fulfilling aspect of financial decision-making.

1. **Understanding Ethical Investing**

Definition and Principles: Delve into the concept of ethical investing, also known as socially responsible investing (SRI), and explore the principles that guide these investment decisions.

2. **Screening Criteria**

Positive and Negative Screens: Learn about the screening criteria used in ethical investing, including positive screens for companies with sustainable practices and negative screens to avoid certain industries or practices.

3. **Case Studies**

Real-world Examples: Showcase case studies of companies that have demonstrated ethical practices and highlight the impact of ethical investing on both financial returns and societal well-being.

Section 2: Sustainable and Responsible Investing

Sustainable investing goes beyond ethical considerations to encompass environmental, social, and governance (ESG) factors. This section explores the broader scope of sustainable and responsible investing.

1. Introduction to ESG Factors
- Breakdown of ESG: Understand the three pillars of ESG investing—Environmental, Social, and Governance—and their relevance to investment decision-making.

2. Corporate Sustainability
- Examining Company Practices: Explore how companies integrate sustainability into their operations, from environmental initiatives to social responsibility programs.

3. Investment Vehicles for Sustainable Investing
- Mutual Funds and ETFs: Investigate investment options that focus on sustainability, including mutual funds and exchange-traded funds (ETFs) with ESG criteria.

Section 3: Balancing Financial Returns with Social and Environmental Impact

Balancing financial returns with the desire for positive social and environmental impact is a key consideration for ethical and sustainable investors. This section addresses the challenges and benefits of finding this equilibrium.

1. Risk and Return Considerations
- Analyzing the Trade-Off: Discuss the common perception of a trade-off between financial returns and ethical considerations, and explore ways to manage this balance.

2. Impact Investing
- Investing for Positive Change: Introduce the concept of impact investing, which aims to generate measurable social and environmental impact alongside financial returns.

3. Long-Term Perspectives
- The Sustainable Advantage: Highlight research suggesting that companies with strong ethical and sustainable practices may exhibit long-term stability and resilience.

Chapter XVI: Financial Apps and Technology

In today's digital age, technology plays a pivotal role in managing personal finances. Various apps and tools are designed to simplify budgeting, investing, and overall financial management. In this chapter, we'll explore the world of financial technology and how it can empower you on your journey to financial literacy.

A. Utilizing Personal Finance Apps and Tools

1. Budgeting Apps:
- **Definition**: Budgeting apps are tools that help you track income, expenses, and savings goals in real-time.
- **Key Features**: Categorizing expenses, setting spending limits, and providing visual representations of your financial data.

Examples: Mint, YNAB (You Need a Budget), and PocketGuard.

2. Investment Platforms:
- **Definition**: Investment apps allow you to invest and manage your portfolio directly from your smartphone.
- **Key Features**: User-friendly interfaces, real-time market updates, and automated investment options.

Examples: Robinhood, Acorns, and Wealthfront.

B. Digital Budgeting and Expense Tracking

1. Benefits of Digital Budgeting:
- **Accuracy**: Real-time tracking helps you make informed decisions based on current financial data.
- **Automation**: Many apps automate expense categorization, saving you time and reducing manual effort.
- **Accessibility**: Access your budget anytime, anywhere, keeping you in control of your finances on the go.

2. Tips for Effective Digital Budgeting:
- **Regular Updates**: Make it a habit to update your budget regularly to reflect changes in income, expenses, and financial goals.
- **Syncing Accounts**: Link your bank accounts and credit cards for seamless transaction tracking.
- **Goal Setting**: Utilize budgeting apps that allow you to set and monitor savings goals for specific objectives.

C. Staying Secure in the Digital Financial Landscape

1. Security Measures:

- **Two-Factor Authentication (2FA)**: Enable 2FA for an extra layer of security when accessing financial apps.
- **Secure Networks**: Avoid accessing financial apps on public Wi-Fi networks to prevent unauthorized access.
- **Regular Updates**: Keep your apps and devices up to date with the latest security patches.

2. Privacy Concerns and Data Protection:

- **Read Privacy Policies**: Understand how apps handle your data and what measures they have in place to protect your privacy.
- **Limit Permissions**: Only grant necessary permissions to apps, minimizing the data they can access.

Conclusion

Financial technology can also help you learn about managing money effectively. Nevertheless, one must be careful with employing those resources and pay particular attention to the issue of security and confidentiality. The integration of these financial apps in your routine will help you make wise financial decision in a rapidly changing technologically driven society.

www.ingramcontent.com/pod-product-compliance
Lightning Source LLC
Chambersburg PA
CBHW080947260726
48661CB00010B/4131